WOMEN *of the* LIGHTS

Candace Fleming

WOMEN *of the* LIGHTS

Candace Fleming

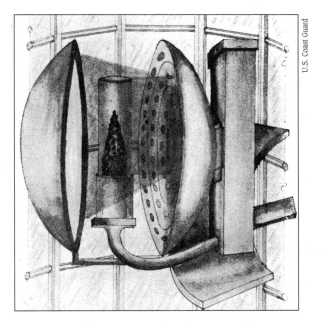

U.S. Coast Guard

ILLUSTRATIONS BY JAMES WATLING

ALBERT WHITMAN & COMPANY • MORTON GROVE, ILLINOIS

For Scott

Title page illustration: Early reflecting-type lamp, used in America in the nineteenth century.

Library of Congress Cataloging-in-Publication Data
Fleming, Candace.
Women of the lights / written by Candace Fleming;
illustrations by James Watling.
p.   cm.
Summary: Chronicles the lives of women lighthouse keepers,
who braved seas and storms, rescued people from icy waters,
and lovingly cared for their lights.
ISBN 0-8075-9165-3
1. Women lighthouse keepers—United States—Juvenile literature.
2. Lighthouses—United States—Juvenile literature.
[1. Lighthouse keepers. 2. Lighthouses. 3. Women—Biography.]
I. Watling, James, ill. II. Title.
VK1023.F53 1996   95-1320
387.1'55'092273—dc20   CIP
[B]   AC

The text is set in Caxton Book.
The illustrations are watercolor.
The design is by Karen A. Yops.

Illustrations copyright © 1996 by James Watling.
Text copyright © 1996 by Candace Fleming.
Published in 1996 by Albert Whitman & Company,
6340 Oakton Street, Morton Grove, IL 60053.
Published simultaneously in Canada by General Publishing,
Limited, Toronto.
Printed in the United States of America.
10 9 8 7 6 5 4 3 2 1

Contents

The Boston Light, erected in 1716, was the first lighthouse built in the American colonies. It was located on Little Brewster Island, Boston Harbor.

Introduction

As long as there have been lighthouses in America, there have been women keeping them. Hannah Thomas was the first. From 1768 to 1786, Hannah lived with her husband, John, on a long finger of land called Gurnet Point. It jutted into Plymouth Bay in the colony of Massachusetts.

Gurnet Point, with its rocky ledges and shallow waters, was a treacherous spot for ships at sea. More than one vessel had been dashed to pieces on the point's sharp rocks, or had run aground in its shallows. Gurnet Point desperately needed a lighthouse to warn sailors of these coastal dangers.

In 1768, the Massachusetts Bay Colony made the Thomases an offer. The colony would rent their land for five shillings a year, build a lighthouse on it, and pay John a salary of two hundred pounds a year to act as its keeper. John agreed, and within the year he and Hannah moved into the new lighthouse. Together they worked to keep the lighthouse operating.

But historic events soon took John away. In 1775, war broke out between Britain and the American colonies. A year later, John marched off to fight for independence. Hannah was left behind to tend the lighthouse.

Tending Gurnet Point's twin towers was not an easy

task. At the top of each tower was a wooden-framed, glass-paned box called a lantern. Inside each lantern were two lamps which burned whale oil. Each of these lamps used four large wicks (cords placed directly into fuel). The lamps were often difficult to keep lit.

At least three times each night, Hannah would climb the towers. She had to trim, or cut down, the wicks to keep them from smoking. She had to refill the lamps with whale oil to keep them burning. And she had to wipe soot from the lanterns' glass to keep the light bright and visible for ships at sea.

It was exhausting work. Yet Hannah kept the lights burning through thick fog, swirling snow, and raging storms.

As it turned out, Hannah also kept the lights burning through enemy attack. During the Revolutionary War, hostile British ships cruised up and down the American coast, seizing colonial vessels. Lighthouses like Hannah's aided the colonial ships by guiding them into safe harbors and inlets. The British believed that if these guiding lights could be destroyed, colonial ships would be easier to attack.

Fearing for the safety of their lighthouse, colonists gathered together and built a makeshift fort around its base. They hoped their efforts would protect the lighthouse.

In 1778, a battle between British sailors and the Gurnet Point residents took place directly below the lighthouse towers. In the heat of the battle, a wild shot from a British cannon struck the walls of Hannah's lighthouse. The shot left a hole, but the lights went undamaged.

How did Hannah feel while this battle raged at her front door? We can only guess. Sadly, no diaries, letters, logbooks, or other mementos of Hannah's time at the Gurnet Point Lighthouse remain. No one bothered to save them, or any other early lighthouse keepers' records, for that matter. Apparently, they weren't considered important enough.

Because of this lack of recordkeeping, little else is known of Hannah's life. No one knows what became of Hannah after she left the lighthouse, or if her husband ever returned from the war, or even when she died. The story of America's first woman lighthouse keeper simply ends.

It wasn't until 1830, more than fifty years after the Gurnet Point battle, that records of keepers began to be preserved. In that year the newly appointed head of the United States Lighthouse Service, Stephen Pleasonton, made sweeping changes in the way lighthouses were run. The first and most important of these was recordkeeping.

Pleasonton demanded that lighthouse records be maintained. All names of keepers would be listed. Logbooks, registers, written reports, and letters of appoint-ments would be filed systematically with the Lighthouse Service, a division of the Treasury Department, in Washington, D.C. At long last, the stories of keepers and their lighthouses could be told.

And what stories they were! Lighthouse keeping was a perilous job. Keepers needed to handle a boat expertly and forecast weather accurately. They needed to be ready to rescue people from rough waters at a moment's notice. They had to live alone for long periods of time and perform heavy physical labor. And they needed to be tough enough to survive hurricanes, tidal waves, ice storms, and even Indian attacks.

For these reasons, many people believed only able-bodied men could endure the rigors of lighthouse keeping. But many women, like Hannah Thomas, also found it their calling to become keepers. Some of these women were the unofficial light keepers, working beside their husbands and fathers with the same dedication and courage. Most, however, were the official keepers themselves.

The women represented in the following chapters are just a handful of the more than two hundred and fifty women who cared for the United States's lighthouses since 1768. Their stories are based on their own accounts as well as newspapers and magazines of the day and other historical sources.

Chapter 1
The Heroine of Lime Rock

On a summer day in 1869, President Ulysses S. Grant arrived at the Lime Rock Lighthouse. But when the president tried to step from his boat to the shore, he missed. Instead, Grant found himself standing ankle-deep in water.

Aghast, presidential aides and officers splashed to his side. But Grant waved them away. "I have come to see Ida Lewis," he said. "To see her I would get wet up to my armpits."

Ida Lewis dealt with the president's mishap graciously. Ignoring Grant's squishy shoes, she took his arm and led him to her lighthouse. After a long chat in which the president

asked many questions about her life on the tiny island, Ida showed him the lights she had tended for so many nights.

Grant was captivated. He later said that his visit with Ida Lewis had been one of the most interesting events of his life—wet shoes and all!

Idawalley Zorada Lewis was born in 1842, in Newport, Rhode Island. Her father, Captain Hosea Lewis, retired from sea duty when Ida was sixteen years old and moved his wife and four children to the Lime Rock Lighthouse, located on a bleak quarter-acre island three hundred yards off the shore of Newport. But only four months after the family's move, Captain Lewis suffered a stroke which left him permanently disabled.

For a time, Captain Lewis's wife managed to care for both the lighthouse and her sick husband. Then, tragedy struck again. The Lewises' youngest daughter, Harriet, became seriously ill. Mrs. Lewis found it impossible to nurse her sick daughter and husband, take care of her two younger children, and tend the lighthouse. The Lewis family had no other choice but to hand over the responsibilities of running the lighthouse to their eldest daughter, Ida.

Sixteen-year-old Ida accepted her new job gladly. In running and maintaining the lighthouse, she found a freedom she had never known before. No longer was she limited to the traditional female roles of cooking and housekeeping. Now, Ida was doing a man's job.

Ida had many talents suited to life at a lighthouse. She was, reportedly, the best swimmer in Newport. She was also a hard worker and an outstanding boatswoman.

HARPER'S WEEKLY

A JOURNAL OF CIVILIZATION

VOL. XIII.—No. 657.]   NEW YORK, SATURDAY, JULY 31, 1869.   [SINGLE COPIES, TEN CENTS. $4.00 PER YEAR IN ADVANCE.

Entered according to Act of Congress, in the Year 1869, by Harper & Brothers, in the Clerk's Office of the District Court of the United States, for the Southern District of New York.

Ida Lewis, the heroine of Lime Rock

Ida's younger brother, Hosea, once said of his sister, "She knew how to handle a boat, hold onto the wind, and fight a gale better than any man I ever saw wet an oar. And do it too, when the sea was breaking over her."

Ida's boat-handling skills were put to the test. On a windy September day in 1858, Ida spotted four boys sailing between Lime Rock and Fort Adams, an army base across the bay from Newport. Ida kept her eyes on the boys. They acted unsure of their direction, and they couldn't operate the sailing equipment. To Ida, the boys looked like inexperienced sailors.

She was right. A few moments later, one boy foolishly shinnied up the mast. The boat capsized, tossing them all into the sea.

Ida hurried to her boat. She quickly rowed to the scene, but avoided the boys' desperate grasps. Instead, she drew ahead. She pulled each boy aboard from the back of the boat. By keeping the stern towards them, she prevented the boat from overturning.

The boys didn't thank Ida for their rescue. And they didn't tell anyone about the heroic young woman who saved their lives.

But Ida didn't care. She considered the rescues to be simply a part of her job. In later years, Ida, in her modest way, said about that first rescue, "I did not think the matter worth talking about and never gave it a second thought."

During the next eleven years, Ida saved the lives of eight more men. But people didn't learn about these exploits, either, until 1869, when a grateful soldier told the local newspaper how Ida had saved his life.

The soldier had gone sailing for the day with a friend from Fort Adams. The men knew little about sailing, so they hired a teenage boy to supervise the trip. Too late, the men learned that their young guide was not as experienced a sailor as he claimed to be.

By afternoon, the three were hopelessly lost. To make matters worse, an icy March rain began to fall. The soldiers' inexperience, the boy's ineptness, and the rain resulted in disaster. The skiff overturned, dumping all three into the choppy waves.

The boy was swept away by the current and drowned. The horrified soldiers clung to the slippery sides of the boat. They cried over and over for help.

Ida, at home with a bad cold, heard the soldiers' cries. Without bothering to cover her head or even put on her shoes, Ida raced to her lifeboat. Her brother Rudolph followed.

The soldiers saw the boat coming towards them. Their cries for help turned to cries of joy. Then one of the men recognized the rower as a woman. His hopes were dashed. He didn't believe a woman could pull them from the water. "However," the man later told the newspaper, "I soon changed my mind."

As Ida drew near the men, Rudolph reached down and tried to pull one of the soldiers over the side.

"No, Rudolph!" Ida shouted. "We'll capsize!"

As always, Ida rowed ahead of the soldiers and pulled them aboard from the back of the boat.

One of the indebted soldiers told the incident to the local press. A reporter from the *New York Herald-Tribune* read the story and was inspired to write a feature article on Ida.

Overnight, Ida became a celebrity. The Life Saving Benevolent Association awarded her a silver medal and one hundred dollars. The soldiers at Fort Adams collected two hundred eighteen dollars for Ida. And the owner of a steamer company granted Ida a lifetime pass on any of his passenger ships.

There were other awards as well. That Fourth of July, the citizens of Newport presented Ida with an elaborate mahogany rowboat complete with red velvet cushions and gold-plated oarlocks.

Dressed in her everyday brown poplin dress, blushing with self-consciousness, Ida stood in her new boat. But she was too shy to make a speech. Instead, she asked Colonel Thomas Wentworth Higginson, a friend of her father's, to talk for her.

"Ida Lewis has never made a speech before," Colonel Higginson told the crowd. "She doesn't plan to now. But if she was to speak to you, she might tell you that she is the most courageous girl in all America."

Just weeks after Newport's celebration, Ida's picture appeared on the cover of *Harper's Weekly*, a well-known national magazine. From coast to coast, Americans read about Ida's heroism. The article noted that Ida's rescue of the drowning men "was a most daring feat, and required the courage and perseverance such as few males ever are possessed of."

Ida in the Rescue, *the boat given to her by the citizens of Newport*

Letters poured into Ida's mailbox. From as far away as Australia and London, people wrote to Ida to tell her how much they admired her. Some letter writers admired Ida so much they proposed marriage. One would-be husband wrote, "I will make you the proudest lady in the world." Ida never wrote back.

But the author of the letter persisted. One day, he unexpectedly turned up at the Lime Rock Lighthouse. Ida met him wearing a rumpled housedress and the odd-shaped slippers she wore when doing lighthouse chores. She did not invite the eager suitor inside. Rather, she suggested they row in her boat for a while.

The young man turned out to be a clumsy rower. He

did not like the rocking motion of the waves or the salt water that sprayed his new suit. Once back on shore, the man leapt from the rowboat. He left Lime Rock as quickly as he had come.

Because of her growing fame, Ida no longer lived in solitude. Almost one hundred visitors a day arrived at Lime Rock to get a glimpse of their heroine. Among these visitors was Susan B. Anthony, the woman suffrage leader. Anthony praised Ida for her role in "promoting the causes of women."

All this fanfare, however, did not change Ida's modest demeanor. She devoted her attention to her family and to taking care of her lighthouse. The *Newport Daily News* visited Ida at Lime Rock and reported:

> Ida met us at the door, as different a being from our expectations of a possibly over-flattered and consequently spoiled girl might lead us to anticipate. There was neither assumption or affectation in her manner. She apologized for her everyday work garb saying frankly that she was trying to help her mother get a little washing done.

In 1870, Ida did something spontaneous and totally out of character. She married Captain William H. Wilson, a sailor and fisherman from Black Rock, Connecticut, and moved with him to his home on the mainland.

Ida's marriage was not a happy one. No one knows why for sure. But Captain Wilson's disappearance from Ida's life probably had something to do with the Lime Rock

Lighthouse. After her marriage, she was separated from her beloved lighthouse. It must have been a difficult change for her.

When Ida's father died in 1872, the government officially offered the lighthouse post to Ida. Whether Ida left her husband to return to Lime Rock, or whether she returned to Lime Rock because her husband left her, is unknown. We do know, however, that Ida moved back to the lighthouse. Her brother Rudolph became her assistant.

One of Ida's last daring rescues came in February 1881. Two soldiers from Fort Adams foolishly decided to walk across the half-frozen Newport Harbor. But the men's weight was too much for the weak ice. It cracked open, and the soldiers fell into the frigid water below.

From the warmth of the lighthouse, Ida heard the drowning men's cries. Springing from her chair, she grabbed a clothesline and raced out the door. Rudolph hurried after her.

But Ida was faster. Disregarding the danger to herself, she ran across the soft, cracking ice and tossed her line to the soldiers. With incredible strength, she managed to haul out one of the men before Rudolph even arrived at the scene. Together, sister and brother rescued the second soldier.

Where did Ida get this strength? When asked, she once replied, "I don't know. I ain't particularly strong. The Lord Almighty gives it to me when I need it, that's all."

On October 20, 1911, Ida filled the lamps with oil, trimmed the wicks, and lit the lights for the last time. That

Ida, in her later years, with canine companions

night, at the age of sixty-nine, she suffered a severe stroke. She died four days later.

Ida's death made national news. In Newport, shopkeepers closed their doors the morning of the funeral. The Trinity Church could not hold all the people who came to pay their last respects. Said the Reverend Stanley C. Hughes in his eulogy, "Ida Lewis was the most remarkable woman Newport ever produced."

Ida was indeed remarkable. But it wasn't just her rescues or fame that made her special. It was also her devotion to the lighting of the lanterns at dusk, the trimming of the wick, and the countless other rituals she performed.

Said Ida, "The light is my child and I know it needs me, even when I'm sleeping."

Chapter 2
"Mind the Light, Katie"

On a cold March day in 1885, a Lighthouse Service boat ploughed through the choppy waves of New York Harbor. Although an icy rain had begun to fall, Captain John Walker and his wife, Kate, stood on deck. Captain Walker had just been appointed as the new keeper at Robbins Reef Lighthouse, and he and his wife, along with their children, Jacob and Mary, were anxious to get a glimpse of their new home.

But Kate's first sight of the lighthouse caused her heart to sink. "It looked like the loneliest place on earth," she later said.

Robbins Reef Lighthouse was indeed lonely. Because it was situated in the middle of the harbor, two miles from land, few people bothered to travel to the lighthouse. Just the sight of the waves gnawing at the brown-and-white tower was enough to chase away anyone's thoughts of a visit. Besides, landing at the lighthouse was truly dangerous. There was no pier or quiet inlet to make arrival at the station easy. Instead, visitors had to step directly from the pitching boat to a vertical steel ladder mounted on the lighthouse's base.

As Kate clung to the wet metal rungs that first day, she must have been frightened of tumbling into the foaming water below. Slowly, carefully, she climbed fifty-four feet straight up to the front door of her new home.

The door opened, and Kate stepped onto the main floor of the keeper's living quarters where she discovered an odd, doughnut-shaped kitchen and dining area built around the lighthouse's tall iron tower. A staircase leading to the second floor revealed two small bedrooms and a parlor. Each of these rooms was painted a lifeless gray color. The wooden floorboards were bare, the woodwork was dusty, and the few sticks of furniture were mismatched and in need of repair.

Surveying her new home, Kate must have felt as gloomy as the lighthouse appeared. "Everywhere I look makes me feel lonesome and blue," she told Captain Walker.

Kate continued to feel "lonesome and blue" for weeks after her arrival. She disliked the lighthouse's concrete and steel and longed for trees, flowers, and grass. Once she even decided to leave the lighthouse but changed her mind when she realized how unhappy Captain Walker would be without his family. Said Kate about her first weeks at Robbins Reef Lighthouse, "I refused to unpack my trunks at first, but gradually, a little at a time, I unpacked. After a while, they were all unpacked and I stayed on."

Certainly, Kate never planned on living in a lighthouse. Born in northern Germany, she had sailed to America with her seven-year-old son, Jacob, after the death of her first husband. Although she could not speak any English, she was determined to make a new life for them in America.

They arrived in their new country in 1883. Kate and Jacob made their way to Sandy Hook, New Jersey, where Kate found a job waitressing at a seaside inn.

But Kate found more than a job at Sandy Hook. She also found Captain John Walker, keeper of the Sandy Hook Lighthouse.

Captain Walker offered to give the black-haired, gray-eyed Kate English lessons. Kate accepted, and soon their lessons together blossomed into love. The couple married, and Kate and Jacob moved into the Sandy Hook Lighthouse.

Life at the Sandy Hook Lighthouse was a pleasant one. Not only did Kate's English improve, but she learned to assist Captain Walker in his many lighthouse duties. She made a number of friends and planted a garden where vegetables and flowers grew in abundance. There was also an addition to the Walker family— Mary Walker was born in December 1884.

But Kate's days at the Sandy Hook Lighthouse ended too soon. In January 1885, Captain Walker received notice that the Lighthouse Service had transferred him to Robbins Reef.

Kate tried to make the best of it at the Robbins Reef Lighthouse. She painted the kitchen walls a cheerful blue. She wallpapered the parlor and added a colorful rug. She even filled the windowsill with the flowers she missed so much.

But although Kate could brighten up the inside of the lighthouse, there was little she could do about her isolation. Often she would stare at the New York City skyline from the lantern room. It made her feel even more alone to know that just a few miles away stood the most crowded city in the world, and yet no one came to visit the Walkers at all.

So Kate turned to her family for company. On clear days, she took Mary and Jacob for walks around and around the small base of the tower. As they strolled, Kate taught the children their alphabet, their numbers, and the names of the birds floating overhead. On stormy days, she entertained the children with games of hide-and-seek and dress-up. Once the three of them even staged a play with Captain Walker serving as an audience of one. And each night, the family gathered around the warm glow of the parlor stove, reading aloud or listening to Captain Walker relive his adventures on the sea.

As the months passed, so did Kate's loneliness. She

*Isolated and uninviting, Robbins Reef Lighthouse sits off
Staten Island in New York Harbor.*

began to love her harbor-locked lighthouse and started to think of it as home.

But one morning in 1886, Kate watched helplessly as her cozy world collapsed. For several days, Captain Walker had suffered from a bad cold. On April 15, his cold developed into pneumonia. A frantic Kate signaled by flare for help, and soon a hospital boat arrived at Robbins Reef. As Captain Walker was being carried to the boat, he touched Kate's hand and whispered, "Mind the light, Katie." Two days later, he died.

Kate did mind the light. She stayed and tended it, only leaving the lighthouse on the afternoon of her husband's funeral. Even then, she was back at her job by nightfall.

Although the Lighthouse Service had a willing and competent keeper in Kate Walker, it began searching for a replacement. The service believed it needed a man to run the lighthouse. Several potential keepers came to look over the job, but each decided that Robbins Reef was too remote for him. Finally, with no one willing to take the position, the Lighthouse Service had little choice but to appoint Kate as keeper.

Captain Walker's death and Kate's appointment changed her life drastically. She no longer had time to play games, stage dramas, or read aloud. There were just too many lighthouse chores. Said Kate, "There is plenty to do in a lighthouse besides keeping the light burning. Each day there is a log to keep where you must post everything, from the amount of oil consumed to the state of the weather. And every day the brass must be polished and the lens cleaned.

Besides, the keepers must keep the place shining with new paint."

With the coming of dark, Kate lit the lamps located at the top of the tower. Two or three times each night, she returned to make sure the lamps were still burning. She trimmed the wicks and refilled the lamps with whale oil if necessary.

While there, Kate also checked for ice forming on the lantern room windows. Ice, she knew, cut down on the light's visibility. Frequently, Kate braved winter gales and sub-zero temperatures to chip and scrape at the panes of glass.

All the while, Kate kept a constant lookout for fog. If a sudden fog rolled in, Kate hurried to the basement to start the steam engine that powered the fog siren. Often the cantankerous engine stalled. Then Kate pounded with a hammer on a hand-operated bell, sometimes for hours, until the fog cleared.

And was Kate's work done when the sun came up? Hardly. There were daytime chores to do—shining brass, dusting machinery, checking motors, repairing wind and water damage, sweeping stairs, and polishing the Fresnel lens.

The Fresnel, introduced in 1840, was a circular glass lens which surrounded the lamp and looked much like a giant beehive. This lens, with prisms at the top and bottom and thick magnifying glass in the middle, created a concentrated beam of light that was far more powerful than earlier lamps and reflectors.

The Fresnel lens presented new problems for light keepers. The lens's fragile glass had to be cleaned and polished with special dusters and spirits of wine. The lens turned on a large clockwork mechanism driven by hand-cranked weights hanging inside the lighthouse tower. The clockwork gears required careful oiling and periodic winding.

Despite Kate's long hours, she still managed to get Jacob and Mary to school. Each morning, Kate rowed the children two miles to Staten Island, where a government school was located.

In her years at the lighthouse, Kate had become a strong, skilled boatswoman. Because of this, most of the morning trips to Staten Island went smoothly. But sometimes the unpredictability of the weather even caught the sea-wise Kate off guard.

"I never rowed the children to Staten Island when there was the slightest sign of rain," Kate once told a visitor. "But even with that start, I have come back a few hours later through terrible storms. Once it took three hours to row from the Staten Island docks. A ferry boat threw a line to me and towed me as close to the lighthouse as they dared. While I climbed the ladder, I was covered from head to foot with a coating of ice. The spray from the waves froze as it fell on me."

Back inside the warm lighthouse, Kate removed her wet clothing and found her woolen socks frozen solid. She cut the socks from her feet with the special ivory-handled scissors she used to trim the wicks.

Because of her years of isolation at the lighthouse, the once-sociable Kate eventually found herself unable to cope with the hustle and bustle of New York City. Although she could see the city from her lantern room, she no longer wanted to visit there. Said Kate in later years, "I am in fear of the place. The streetcars bewilder me and I am afraid of automobiles. Why, a fortune wouldn't tempt me to get into one of those things." This from a woman who often rescued fishermen from the frothing tides that ripped around her lighthouse!

Kate has been credited with saving between fifty and seventy-five people. But the rescue Kate remembered most was that of a little Scottie dog.

One evening in 1901, the emergency gun sounded on Governors Island. Kate heard the warning. Knowing the gun was fired only if there was a shipwreck, she hurried down the lighthouse ladder and into her rowboat.

She quickly rowed to the scene of the wreck, searching the dark water for survivors. But all she found was floating debris. Discouraged, Kate headed back towards the lighthouse. Suddenly, a near-dead dog appeared on the end of her oar.

Kate snatched the dog from the frigid water and wrapped him in a blanket she kept stowed in her boat. She rowed swiftly back to her lighthouse where she rubbed the dog vigorously with the blanket and poured hot coffee down his throat.

The dog recovered. By the next morning, he was jumping and prancing about the lighthouse. He was so

Kate Walker at Robbins Reef

devoted to his rescuer that he followed Kate everywhere, even up the tall spiral staircase that led to the lantern room.

Kate became attached to the dog, too. But she knew she couldn't keep him at the lighthouse. Regulations forbade having pets on lighthouse property. So Kate reported her find to the authorities.

A week later, the ship's captain arrived at the lighthouse to claim his dog. The little dog appeared to weep as Kate handed him down the lighthouse ladder.

"It is strange," Kate later recalled, "that one of the pleasantest memories I have of my more than thirty years in the lighthouse should be the loving gratitude of a little dog."

Kate ended her years at Robbins Reef Lighthouse in 1919. At the age of seventy-seven, she retired to a small cottage with a garden on Staten Island. She still lived in isolation, but she no longer considered it a hardship. "There is so much you think that isn't needful to say," she once explained to a visitor.

In the weeks before her death on February 5, 1931, Kate was sometimes seen standing outside her cottage, gazing towards the Robbins Reef Lighthouse. Perhaps she was remembering her many years there. Perhaps she was recalling her many rescues. Or perhaps she was still fulfilling her promise to "Mind the light, Katie."

Chapter 3
The Lady on the Lake

Lake Michigan is as violent and unpredictable as any ocean. Jagged rocks and sandbars line its shores. Furious squalls whip up at a moment's notice. Churning waves and dangerous undercurrents are common. All who travel on, or live by, the lake have a grudging respect for its power. For these and other reasons, Lake Michigan has gained the nickname "inland sea."

So it was no wonder citizens of Michigan City, Indiana, snorted in disbelief when, in January 1861, the name of their new lighthouse keeper was announced.

A woman, they must have thought, it's impossible. How can some fragile female undertake such a perilous job? She won't last a month.

But that fragile female proved them all wrong. Harriet Colfax tended the Michigan City Lighthouse for almost fifty years and did it with such faithfulness that Great Lakes sailors dubbed her lighthouse "Old Faithful."

Harriet's past life never indicated that she would become a lighthouse keeper. This well-educated, genteel lady first worked with her brother at Michigan City's newspaper and later gave music lessons. A petite woman with light brown hair and trusting gray eyes, Harriet loved fancy clothes, parties, and trips to Chicago.

No one knows exactly why Harriet suddenly decided to leave her pleasant life in town to isolate herself at the Michigan City Lighthouse. Town gossips claimed she had fallen head-over-heels in love and that when the romance did not work out, she begged her cousin, Schuyler Colfax, to find her a job far, far away.

Is this story true? No one knows for sure. What is known is that Harriet did ask her cousin for a job. He found her one.

Schuyler Colfax was the vice president of the United States and could have gotten Harriet almost any job she wanted. At that time, it was legal for a person holding political office to appoint relatives and special friends to government jobs. This privilege resulted in what was called the patronage system. Elected officials filled government offices, from local postal clerk to tax collector, with their

The Michigan City Lighthouse, built in 1858, captured in a photograph taken around the turn of the century.

personal acquaintances. Since lighthouse keeping was also a government job, it was a simple matter for Vice President Colfax to appoint Harriet. It didn't matter that Harriet had never taken care of a lighthouse before. She didn't have to pass a test or prove that she could handle the duties. Vice President Colfax's recommendation alone assured her the job.

Harriet accepted her cousin's offer. In March 1861, she

packed her personal belongings and with her lifelong companion, Anne Hartwell, moved to her new home on the shore of Lake Michigan.

Harriet soon discovered that life as a lighthouse keeper was much different than teaching music or writing the town's society column. Harriet's new job required her to keep two lights burning.

The first of these was located in a beacon at the end of a half-mile long pier. Harriet made that trip twice daily, first to light and then to extinguish the lamp. The trip was grueling enough in the summer when the wind gathered into a blustery fist that pounded her from all sides. But in the winter, the trip down the long pier was nothing short of dangerous. Then Harriet slipped and struggled along the icy wooden planks, a vial of warmed oil in one hand and a cleaned lamp in the other. Many times, she arrived at the beacon only to discover that the oil had already cooled and congealed. She would fight her way back to shore, reheat the lard oil on her kitchen stove, and set out on her harrowing journey again.

In addition to the beacon at the end of the pier, Harriet also tended the main light, which projected from the roof of her house. Harriet found this light much easier to care for. She simply climbed the winding stairs from her kitchen to the tower and lit the lamp.

Still, the main light presented its own problems. During the migratory seasons, in fall and spring, the light attracted flocks of birds. Blinded by the light's glare, the birds dashed themselves against the glass lantern panes. They fluttered to the lamproom floor, some stunned, others with broken wings or necks. Harriet spent hours caring for the birds whose injuries could be mended until they could fly away.

The main light also attracted thousands of moths. These insects hovered like clouds around the tower. Harriet often amused herself by identifying the many species or counting the different colors on their wings.

Harriet's working day varied from four or five hours to more, and her tasks were more difficult in the winter than in the summer. In the winter, the lamps had to be lit as early as three-fifteen P.M. and not extinguished until eight o'clock the next morning. During these hours the ever-faithful Harriet refused to sleep. Instead, she cleaned windows, swept floors, chopped wood for her kitchen stove, and updated her logbook.

Day after day, year after year, Harriet followed this routine. Then on October 14, 1886, the rhythm was broken.

A fierce storm began to blow, and darkness fell early. Armed with oil and lamp, Harriet struggled towards the lamp at the end of the pier and into the worst storm that ever raged along the coast of Lake Michigan.

Blinded by ice and snow, Harriet stumbled along the frozen planks. The shrieking wind pummeled her. The slippery pier tripped her. The mountainous waves lashed against the pilings and woodwork until the timbers groaned. With heart pounding, Harriet groped along until she came to the beacon. Battling the wind, she fought open the door and climbed into the shelter of the tower.

Lighting the lamp took only a few minutes. But by the

time Harriet stepped back outside, the storm had increased its fury. The beacon staircase quaked beneath her feet, and the tower swayed in a wind that sounded like the ripping of a thousand giant sails. "For the first time," Harriet later said, "I was scared almost to fainting."

Luckily for Harriet, she didn't faint. She managed to stumble back to shore, reaching its safety just as a terrific crash splintered the air. Harriet looked back and saw the beacon tower, as it was later described by a Chicago newspaper, "like some big meteor, whirl in an arc through the livid night, and fall hissing into the lake." Harriet realized she had barely escaped with her life.

All that blizzardy night, while the storm screamed, Harriet burned the light in the main tower more brightly. She searched the storm-lashed waves for signs of ships. And she prayed for the safety of any sailor out on such a night.

When daylight came, Harriet hurried outside to inspect the damage. It was worse than she had expected. The tower was gone. The pier was gone. And the shore was strewn with wreckage.

Said Harriet, "I have seen many storms. But never one like that. I was sorry to lose the old beacon in spite of all the trouble and danger it gave me, for I was getting fond of it, and it was a great help to sailors who didn't know the old harbor structures."

The beacon and pier were not replaced, and Harriet's duties were reduced to caring for the main light only. But as the years passed, even this job became too difficult for the aging Harriet. Eventually she hired a helper to carry the heavy lamp and oil up the lighthouse stairs. But she still insisted on trimming the wicks and lighting the lamp herself. "None but me has done it," Harriet once told a newspaper reporter. "I love the lamp in the lighthouse, and the work. They are the habit, the home, everything dear I have known for so long."

Sadly, Harriet's home and habit were about to undergo drastic changes. In 1904, the Lighthouse Board built a new pierhead lighthouse and equipped it with the most modern

Harriet Colfax

technology of the day—steam engines, boiler furnaces, newfangled foghorns. Gone was the need for wick trimming, lard oil, and the little lighthouse that Harriet lived in. Harriet's home was converted into a cottage, and the tower and lenses removed and placed in the new lighthouse.

Gone also was the need for Harriet. The new lighthouse, with its elaborate equipment, needed someone knowledge-able about repairing and maintaining heavy machinery. The Lighthouse Board retired Harriet and replaced her with a young man named Thomas Armstrong.

Harriet watched these changes wistfully. "It can never be the same after my old light is gone. I don't know how I will sleep knowing it is out and I cannot light it again."

On October 12, 1904, Harriet lit the lamps and wrote in her logbook for the last time. Her entry reads, "Fair, warm wind, smokey atmosphere. Received another call from Mr. Armstrong, my successor."

And the next day, October 13, Keeper Armstrong made his first entry. It reads, "The retiring keeper left this station at four P.M. with all her personal effects."

Harriet, still accompanied by her friend, Anne, retired to a quiet home in town. Just five months later, she died at the age of eighty.

Chapter 4
The Grandes Dames
of Lightkeeping

In the late 1890s, Point Pinos Lighthouse, on
California's Monterey Peninsula, was a center of culture
and sophistication. Writers, artists, and other prominent
members of Monterey society scrambled for an invitation
to the elegant private dinner parties given by the lighthouse
keeper. After all, Emily Fish was the "grande dame" of
polite society.

Emily's background was one of wealth, education, and high social position. At sixteen, she traveled from her hometown of Albion, Michigan, to far-off China. There she joined her older sister, Juliet, and Juliet's husband, Dr. Melancthon Fish. It was during her stay in China that Juliet gave birth to a baby girl, also named Juliet. But the joyous event soon turned to tragedy. Emily's sister died, leaving baby Juliet motherless and Dr. Fish without a wife.

Eventually, Emily herself married Dr. Fish. And although Juliet was in actuality Emily's niece, Emily raised and loved the child as her own daughter.

The Fish family traveled to Oakland, California, where Dr. Fish opened a private medical practice and became a prominent citizen. Emily became a social whirlwind. Juliet grew up and married a dashing, distinguished naval officer named Henry Nichols. The wedding was the social event of the season. Surely none of the guests would have guessed that Emily and Juliet Fish would end up as lighthouse keepers.

But in 1890, Dr. Fish died. Emily was left wondering what she could do with her future. The answer came from her son-in-law, Commander Nichols.

One evening after dinner, Commander Nichols mentioned that the keeper at Point Pinos Lighthouse was retiring. Emily's curiosity was aroused. She bombarded her son-in-law with questions. What were a keeper's duties? How much were keepers paid? Could lighthouse keepers have servants? Commander Nichols answered Emily's questions in detail.

And Emily made up her mind. Even though she had absolutely no lighthouse experience, she asked for the job. Since Commander Nichols served as the inspector of the twelfth district of the Lighthouse Service, he made sure Emily received the position.

Emily arrived at her lighthouse home in 1893. She was fifty years of age and accustomed to a life of leisure and comfort. One might have expected her to hop back into her carriage the minute she laid eyes on the lighthouse. After all, what Emily found was a drab, gray building standing on a treeless sand lot.

But Emily didn't flinch at this dismal sight. She determined that hers would be a stylish, comfortable lighthouse. Immediately, she set about transforming Point Pinos.

The inside was cleaned, polished, and painted. She added expensive furniture, fine paintings, and shelves of leather-bound books. Flower-filled crystal vases stood on mahogany tables. Persian rugs covered the scuffed floorboards. For the first time in Point Pinos's history, the rooms glowed with beauty.

Outside, Emily and her Chinese servant, Que, improved the grounds. They covered the sand with rich, dark topsoil and planted cypress trees and grass and other ground coverings. They laid out a garden, which soon blossomed into a mass of fragrant flowers. They added a gravel walk leading to the front door and an ornamental fountain that splashed day and night in the back.

Not content with the government-issue livestock provided by the Lighthouse Board, Emily brought her own

*Emily Fish, standing beside the entrance of the renovated
and refurbished Point Pinos Lighthouse.*

animals—thoroughbred horses, blooded Holstein cows, and
even her pedigreed French poodles.

But Emily did more than redecorate. She took her lighthouse responsibilities seriously, knowing it was imperative
that the Point Pinos light function properly. Ship traffic
along the Monterey Peninsula was heavy. Vessels hugged
the coast, stopping at the smallest ports to deliver
passengers, cargo, and mail. Without the lighthouse's
guidance, a ship could easily wreck on the rocky shores.

Emily understood this danger. She tended the wicks and lamps herself and on stormy nights never left the watch-tower in case the flame should go out. She conscientiously kept her logbook updated and always made sure the grounds and machinery were well maintained.

Of course, Emily didn't actually maintain the grounds and machinery herself. She hired laborers to polish brass, paint walls, dust lenses, and wash windows. Records show she was a tough taskmaster. Emily hired more than thirty different men during her twenty-one years as keeper. Most of these men she fired for "incompetence."

The hiring of these laborers freed Emily's time for more social endeavors. During her years at Point Pinos, Emily served on various committees, organized charity balls, and attended many social events. When the Spanish-American War broke out in 1898, Emily convinced her friends to form a Monterey-Pacific Grove chapter of the American Red Cross. She served on its first executive committee.

But the Spanish-American War brought Emily more than a new committee to chair. It also brought the sad news that her son-in-law, Commander Nichols, had died. No one knows how Emily consoled her daughter, Juliet. But perhaps Emily advised Juliet to take up lighthouse keeping as an antidote against grief. A few years later, Juliet became the keeper of the Angel Island Lighthouse, located in San Francisco Bay.

On April 18, 1906, near the end of Emily's watch, the horses in the barn began pounding on the floor. The Holsteins mooed wildly. Even the well-behaved poodles barked and raced about excitedly. Emily was puzzled. Usually such behavior from the animals meant a storm was brewing. But that couldn't be. The last few hours before dawn had been beautiful, the moonlight dancing on the surf and the drifting clouds making unusual patterns of light and dark as they scuttled across the moon.

Emily headed for the watchroom where she sat by the window and waited for Que to bring her breakfast tray. She was still pondering the animals' odd behavior when the servant arrived. Emily told him of her concerns.

But Que never had a chance to answer. Suddenly, the earth quivered, then quaked. A crackling, tinkling sound of shattering glass came from the tower.

Fighting to keep their balance, Emily and Que rushed up the crazily rocking stairs. Just as they arrived in the lantern room, the flame in the lamp made a strange whooshing sound, then shot several feet into the air. The two fought desperately to control the dangerous flame as the earth continued to quake.

When at last the earthquake ended, Emily assessed the damage. The lens prisms were scratched. The tower was cracked, and the wooden outbuildings had been wrenched from their foundations.

Emily hurried to report the damage to her district lighthouse office in San Francisco. But to her dismay, she learned that all telegraph, telephone, and train service beyond Salinas, ten miles away, was impossible.

Desperate for news, Emily hurried into the nearby town of Pacific Grove where she knew the navy destroyer *Prible* had just arrived. The ship's captain told her the news. San Francisco had been devastated by an earthquake. He and his crew were headed there now, under navy orders to preserve the peace. As Emily watched the *Prible* sail away, she worried about her daughter, Juliet, in San Francisco Bay. Was she safe?

On that fateful morning, Juliet had just finished her final check of the lighthouse machinery and was headed to bed when a strange rumbling stopped her. Looking across the bay towards San Francisco, she was astonished to see waterfront buildings collapsing.

Unable to believe her eyes, Juliet snatched up her field glasses and peered through them. Now, all too clearly, she could see the devastation—shops and factories reduced to rubble, homes crumbled, and then, fire. Shocked, Juliet watched as the fire grew, hungrily leaping from building to building, filling the sky with black smoke and hot ashes.

When the earthquake ended, little remained standing in San Francisco. Strangely, Juliet's lighthouse suffered no damage. Soon she heard that the earthquake had damaged towns as far as one hundred miles away. What had happened at Point Pinos?

But Juliet didn't have time to worry. San Francisco Bay had always been a busy waterway, but now the bay bustled with more activity than she had ever seen. Day and night, ships loaded with soldiers and with food, medicine, and other supplies lined up at the bay's entrance. Juliet kept busy lighting lanterns and starting the machinery that operated Angel Island's fog bell.

Emily Fish

But it would be the fog bell, not the earthquake, that later that year would present the biggest challenge for Juliet. San Francisco is notorious for its heavy fogs. One afternoon, less than three months after the earthquake, Juliet watched as a pea-soup-thick fog crept across the bay. Other lighthouse bells were already ringing when Juliet dashed to her fog bell machinery. But the cantankerous machine refused to start.

Looking towards sea, Juliet could just make out the silhouette of a sailing ship headed straight for Angel Island. Unless she did something quickly, the ship would run aground on the island's shores.

Frantically, Juliet grabbed a hammer and pounded on the bell. The ship, hearing the warning, veered clear of the island.

The ship was saved, but the fog remained. Without a mechanical fog bell, Juliet had to pound away manually with the heavy hammer. Hour after hour, she beat on the bell. Her back and legs ached. Her arms felt like rubber. Her fingers were numb from gripping the hammer's handle. Time and again Juliet thought she couldn't go on. Then she would hear an approaching ship and bang away with renewed vigor.

Twenty hours later, the fog lifted. Ill and exhausted, Juliet dropped into bed. But less than two days later, the fog bell once more refused to start. Still not completely recovered from her last ordeal, Juliet again lifted the hammer and pounded away once more. This time the fog lasted fourteen hours.

Eventually, such rigors became too much for Juliet. In 1914 she left Angel Island. She remarried and settled in the hills of Piedmont, a suburb of Oakland. For the next thirty-three years Juliet lived a quiet, private life. She died at age eighty-eight in 1947.

And what of Juliet's indomitable mother, Emily? Coincidentally, Emily also left lighthouse keeping in 1914. She bought a home in Pacific Grove and retired there with her devoted servant, Que. Emily occupied herself growing flowers, serving on local committees, and attending social functions until her death in 1931.

Chapter 5
Other Legendary Ladies of the Light

Unfortunately, it is impossible to tell the stories of all two hundred and fifty women lighthouse keepers. The following pages detail just a few more remarkable women who kept the lights.

On a bitter January night in 1856, seventeen-year-old Abbie Burgess struggled to the top of the Matinicus Rock Lighthouse, located on a tiny island off the coast of Maine. Outside, snow swirled in gale-force winds, and a heavy surf pounded the rocks. Inside, twenty-eight lamps stood waiting to be lit.

Earlier in the day, Abbie's father, Keeper John Burgess, had sailed to the mainland in the family's small dinghy. The Burgess family desperately needed food, and Abbie's sick mother needed medicine. Keeper Burgess expected only to be gone overnight.

Abbie had minded the lights before, but never in such bad weather. Almost before her father's boat sailed out of sight, the wind had veered to the northwest and a heavy snow began to fall. By evening, Matinicus Rock was in the

A young woman tending the lights, as pictured in Harper's Young People: An Illustrated Weekly.

grip of a ferocious winter storm.

All that night, Abbie frantically worked to keep the lights burning. She filled each of the lamps with whale oil and inserted fresh wicks. But because of the cold, the whale oil congealed and the flames simply sputtered and died. Obviously, Abbie could not leave the lamps to burn on their own. All night long, she shivered in the frigid lamproom, nursing the lights along. She could hardly wait for daybreak.

But daybreak only brought more horrifying events. When the now-exhausted Abbie looked out the tower window, she gasped. The sea was rising, covering the island and seeping into the ground floor of the lighthouse. It flooded the Burgesses' living quarters.

Abbie's mother and three younger sisters fled into the tower. As they huddled on the stairs, listening to the storm's destruction, Abbie suddenly remembered the chickens outside in their coop. Their eggs were one of the last sources of food for the family.

"I must try to save the chickens!" Abbie shouted to her mother.

Snatching a basket, Abbie plunged knee-deep into the water and struggled for the door. Opening it, she waited for a break in the rushing waves.

The rollers slowed for a moment, and Abbie saw her chance. The ocean churned and boiled around her as she scooped the four frantic hens into the basket and fought her way back to the lighthouse.

"Oh look! Look there!" screamed Abbie's youngest

sister. "The worst sea is coming!"

A mountain-high wall of water rose behind Abbie as she lunged through the open door. Her sister slammed and bolted it only seconds before a giant wave swept the lighthouse.

"The sea shut out every other sound," Abbie later wrote, "even drowning out our voices." The tidal wave was the storm's last hurrah. By afternoon, the water rolled back, the wind died, and the sea calmed.

Eventually, Keeper Burgess made it back to his family and his lighthouse. He found his wife and daughters gathered around a meager supper of cornmush and eggs.

"I knew I could depend on you, Abbie," he said.

But Abbie wasn't the only teenager to do amazing things while living at a lighthouse. Thirteen years later, on California's Monterey Bay, another teenager, named Laura Hecox, would also make her mark.

Laura's father, Adna Hecox, was the keeper of the Santa Cruz Lighthouse, and his job couldn't have made fifteen-year-old Laura happier. There was no place Laura would rather have been than the windswept shoreline. Here she could satisfy her boundless curiosity about the natural world around her.

Nowadays, Laura would probably have gone to college and become a biologist. But in the nineteenth century, girls were not encouraged to study science. Instead, Laura learned on her own. She attended local lectures on marine life, read books, and wrote to experts about the subjects that interested her. Above all, Laura collected.

She collected rocks and fossils, seashells and birds' nests, seaworms and starfish and plant specimens. If it was interesting or unique, Laura collected it.

Laura's collection of odd and curious artifacts grew to such overwhelming proportions that her father was forced to build several large cases for storage. Before long, he was building even more.

When Laura wasn't clambering over rocks or wading through tide pools, she could be found at her father's side. It was from him that Laura learned lighthouse duties.

The Santa Cruz light was a small one, with only one lamp and lens to maintain. Situated on mild Monterey Bay, the lighthouse saw little bad weather, and shipping accidents were rare. The ease of these duties left Laura plenty of time to collect, categorize, and study after helping with the lighthouse.

So much did Laura learn that by the time she was in her twenties she had become one of the state's foremost authorities on shells, rocks, and birds. Even slugs did not escape Laura's notice. While climbing among the rocks one day, she discovered an as-yet-unnamed species of slug. Excitedly, Laura shared her find with a Cincinnati professor who specialized in slugs.

The professor was so taken with Laura's knowledge that he eventually named the new slug species after her. When Laura heard this news, she laughed and said, "Being named after a slug is not the most glamorous tribute to a woman, but it is a tribute all the same."

Another time, a local student of paleontology and

Laura Hecox

geography was so impressed by Laura's collection of fossils that he named a new species of fossil spindle snail in her honor.

In 1883, Adna Hecox died, and Laura, aged twenty-nine, took over as the official light keeper. With only her elderly mother and herself remaining at the lighthouse, Laura decided to devote an entire room to her collection. She built shelves and carefully arranged her artifacts.

Although Laura never intended to establish a museum, that's exactly what happened. Curious people flocked to the lighthouse. Laura greeted them all warmly and took them on a tour of not only her collection room, but the lighthouse lamproom as well. Soon the Santa Cruz Lighthouse and Museum became a popular tourist attraction.

Eventually, Laura donated her entire collection for exhibit in the Santa Cruz Library. Said Laura of her generous donation, "The children of Santa Cruz may find pleasure in having this collection placed so they may benefit from it. Children are never too young to begin the study of nature's book, and never too old to quit."

Laura Hecox never quit. She continued to study and learn and collect, all the while caring for her lighthouse, until her death in 1919.

Laura Hecox was fortunate to have lived out her days in the lighthouse she loved. But some women's lighthouse careers did not end so peacefully. One keeper in Biloxi, Mississippi, had her career cut short by war.

Mary Reynolds received her appointment as keeper of the Biloxi Lighthouse, on the Gulf of Mexico, in 1854.

Widowed, with several children, Mary was pleased to find a job that not only provided a roof for her family, but a yearly salary of four hundred dollars as well.

But in 1861, the Civil War broke out. The citizens of Biloxi demanded that Mary extinguish her light. They refused to allow any lighthouse to remain working when it might aid Yankee ships.

Mary was deeply disturbed over this turn of events. She was, first and foremost, a lighthouse keeper, sworn to keep the lights burning for all ships at sea—Confederate or Yankee. She received a salary from the Union government. Still, Mary was a Southerner, and therefore a citizen of the newly formed Confederate States of America. The situation was very confusing.

In hopes of clarifying her position, Mary wrote the governor of Mississippi in November 1861. "On the eighteenth of June last," wrote Mary,

> the citizens of Biloxi ordered the light to be extinguished . . . and shortly after others came and demanded the keys of the Light Tower which has ever since remained in the hands of the Company calling themselves, "Home Guards."
>
> At the time they took possession of the Tower, it contained valuable Oil. . . . I have on several occasions seen disreputable characters taking out the oil in bottles. . . . They may also take in the night as no one here appeared to have authority over them.
>
> If you would . . . write . . . orders to have the oil placed under my charge at the dwelling of the Light House I would be very grateful.

I write to you merely as a Light Keeper believing
that injustice has been and is still doing here.

The governor's reply to Mary, if there was one, is
unknown. What is known is that Mary and her family left
the lighthouse. They never returned. The Biloxi light was
dark until the end of the war in 1865, and may have
remained dark until 1866.

With the war's end, the Biloxi Lighthouse was handed
back to the Union government and to a brand-new light
keeper—Perry Younghans. But Mr. Younghans died within
the year. His wife, Maria, took over his responsibilities.

During Maria's first year as the keeper, the lighthouse
tower was painted black. Legend has it that this was done
as a sign of mourning for the assassinated President
Lincoln. Biloxi citizens, stinging from the defeat of the
South, descended on the lighthouse in an angry mob,
demanding the tower be repainted. The Union government
quickly agreed, and the tower was repainted white.

Maria continued on as the Biloxi light keeper for an
impressive fifty-one years. With a career that long, one
would imagine that Maria left behind lots of exciting stories
and loads of historical records. She did not. Only a few
newspaper clippings provide a glimpse into Maria's life at
the lighthouse.

At the time of Maria's death in August 1925, the Biloxi
and Gulfport *Daily Herald* wrote that Maria,

> in the winter of 1870 called her brother-in-law and
> effected through him the rescue of a man being swept
> out to sea about daylight, clinging to an upturned boat;

and during the 1916 storm, when the heavy glass in the lighthouse tower was broken by a large pelican being blown against it, she and her daughter, mindful of the especial need of the light on such a night, replaced the glass temporarily and made the "light to shine" as before, unimpaired.

Obviously, Maria was a dutiful and devoted light keeper. When she retired from her post in 1919, her daughter, Miranda, assumed the keeper position. According to newspaper accounts, Miranda was a beloved citizen of Biloxi. One newspaper noted that, "her unfailing courtesy and dignity gave hundreds of casual visitors to the lighthouse a beautiful memory of her."

Miranda Younghans

In 1926 the Biloxi Lighthouse was electrified. Three years later, Miranda Younghans retired.

Electrification of lighthouses hastened the end of many keepers' careers, especially those of women. After the turn of the century, much of the old-fashioned equipment began to be replaced with more efficient, modern equipment. Now electricity would turn the lens, and a high-watt electric bulb would illuminate it. These advances in technology made lighthouse keeping simple. So much simpler, in fact, that fewer and fewer lighthouses needed live-in keepers. The remaining keeper jobs were usually given to men because it was believed that only men could acquire the skills necessary to repair and operate modern engines and intricate electrical mechanisms. As more lighthouses became electrified, the Lighthouse Service asked women keepers to retire or transferred them to light stations with simpler types of equipment.

Still, one woman keeper proved that females could make the transition from oil to light bulbs.

Fannie Salter arrived in 1923 at the Turkey Point Lighthouse, located at the mouth of the Elk River on Maryland's Chesapeake Bay. Her husband, C. W. Salter, was the official keeper, but like many lighthouse wives before her, Fannie also learned to care for the lighthouse. Turkey Point soon became a place Fannie loved—a place she called home.

When her husband died in 1925, Fannie simply assumed she would continue on at Turkey Point. After all, women had been replacing their husbands as light keepers

---

Fannie Salter and her son, feeding turkeys at Turkey Point Lighthouse.

since the birth of the nation.

But it was no longer that easy. By 1925, the Lighthouse Service had undergone huge changes. People could no longer receive lighthouse jobs simply by having political connections. Now young men, but not young women, were encouraged to join the lighthouse service at the bottom rank and work their way up, gaining the skills and experience necessary to run a modern lighthouse. Applicants for keeper also had to meet specific job requirements and qualifications. One of these job requirements was age.

Although Fannie was only forty-two, the Lighthouse Service told her that the new rules prevented her from succeeding her husband because she was too old. Fannie, the service said, would have to go.

But Fannie Salter had no intention of leaving her home. Instead she wrote to her state senator, insisting that he secure her lighthouse position.

The senator went straight to the top. President Calvin Coolidge himself appointed Fannie to her post.

Like those of women keepers before her, Fannie's days were filled with hard work. She, too, polished brass, painted walls, swept stairs, and kept an eye out for fog. And four or five times each night, she climbed the tower to fill and light the brass oil lamps inside the lens.

But in 1943, electricity arrived at Turkey Point. A one-hundred-watt light bulb replaced the brass lamps. Fannie's nights of backbreaking work and constant worry were over. Her lights now went on with a flip of a wall switch.

Fannie learned to change the electric bulb in the lens

whenever necessary. She made minor repairs on the newly installed electrical plant which turned the lens. And she tinkered with the gasoline-powered engine that now ran her foghorn. When a radio-telephone set was installed at Turkey Point, Fannie taught herself to use it simply by reading the technical manual. Fannie was indeed a modern light keeper.

And she was also the last civilian woman to keep a lighthouse. In 1939, the Lighthouse Service, with all its duties and responsibilities, was handed over to the United States Coast Guard. As part of this changeover, civilian lighthouse keepers were allowed to remain in their positions. But when these keepers reached retirement, they were replaced with Coast Guard personnel.

Six years after this changeover, in 1945, Fannie was asked about her possible retirement. Said Fannie, "I plan to stay as long as the Coast Guard wants me. Perhaps after the war, I'll make other plans."

Just two years later, Fannie left her beloved lighthouse and retired to Baltimore. She was sixty-four.

Fannie's retirement marked the end of an era. From now on, the Coast Guard would oversee America's lighthouses. Some of the lighthouses would be decommissioned, that is, put out of service. Others would undergo technological improvements, such as powerful aerobeams with thousand-watt bulbs, plastic lenses with solar-powered beams, and simple platforms or poles in place of towers. These improvements made the care of lighthouses simpler. Today, a single Coast Guard official can oversee several lighthouses

Fannie Salter, polishing the Fresnel lens at Turkey Point.

just by checking periodically to make sure the equipment is in working order.

American women can no longer be found living and working in their lighthouses. Still, their two hundred years of courage and sacrifice live on. And like the lights they tended, their stories provide inspiration and guidance.

BIBLIOGRAPHY AND SOURCE NOTES

The information contained in this book is based on many sources. In reconstructing the lives of these women, I consulted books, magazine articles, newspaper accounts, logbooks, letters, and interviews. Thoughts and dialogue were not fictionalized, but were taken directly from firsthand accounts. Much fascinating firsthand information was found in the National Archives, Washington, D.C., and in the records of the United States Coast Guard, Washington, D.C. Other helpful organizations providing original documents were the United States Lighthouse Society, San Francisco, California; the Old Lighthouse Museum, Michigan City, Indiana; the Newport Historical Society, Newport, Rhode Island; and the Monterey Historical and Art Association, Monterey, California.

GENERAL HISTORIES

The following books were especially helpful in providing an overview of the history of America's lighthouses as well as detailing the functions and operations of a lighthouse.

Beaver, Patrick. *A History Of Lighthouses*. Secaucus, N.J.: Citadel Press, 1973.

Carse, Robert. *Keepers of the Lights*. New York: Charles Scribner's Sons, 1969.

Gibbons, Gail. *Beacons of Light*. New York: Morrow Junior Books, 1990.

Holland, Francis Ross. *Great American Lighthouses*. Washington, D.C.: Preservation Press, 1989.

Hyde, Charles K. *The Northern Lights*. Lansing, Mich.: Two Peninsula Press, 1986.

Snow, Edward Rowe. *Famous Lighthouses of America.* New York: Dodd, Mead & Company, 1955.

Ziegler, Philip C. *America's Guiding Lights.* Camden, Maine: Down East Books, 1989.

INTRODUCTION

Holland, Francis Ross. *America's Lighthouses: Their Illustrated History Since 1716.* Brattleboro, Vt.: Stephen Grune Press, 1972.

Snow, Edward Rowe. *The Lighthouses of New England.* New York: Dodd, Mead & Company, 1945.

CHAPTER ONE: *The Heroine of Lime Rock*

Bachand, Robert G. *Northeast Lights: Lighthouses and Lightships Rhode Island to Cape May, New Jersey.* Norfolk, Conn.: Seasports Publications, 1989.

Dewire, Elinor. "Beacons from the Past." *Americana* (October 1986).

_____. "Women Lighthouse Keepers." *American History Illustrated* 21 (February 1987).

Gleason, Sarah C. *Kindly Lights.* Boston: Beacon Press, 1991.

Jones, Ray, and Bruce Roberts. *Northern Lighthouses, New Brunswick to the Jersey Shore.* Chester, Conn.: Globe Pequot Press, 1989.

Lists of Lights and Fog Signals. Washington, D.C.: Department of Commerce Printing, 1939.

Thompson, Sue Ellen. "The Light Is My Child." *The Log of Mystic Seaport* 32, no. 3 (Fall 1980).

United States Lighthouse Board: Documents Relating to Lighthouses, 1789–1871. Washington, D.C.: Government Printing Office, 1871.

CHAPTER TWO: *"Mind the Light, Katie"*

Anderson, Hans Christian. *Keepers of the Lights.* New York: Greenberg Publishers, 1955.

Dewire, Elinor. "Women Lighthouse Keepers." *American History Illustrated* 21 (February 1987).

Duffy, Francis James. "Lights of the Port of New York." *Sea Frontiers* 31 (November–December 1985).

Gallant, Clifford. "Mind The Light, Katie." *The Keeper's Log* (Summer 1987).

Holland, Francis Ross. *America's Lighthouses: Their Illustrated History Since 1716.* Brattleboro, Vt.: Stephen Grune Press, 1972.

"Kept House Nineteen Years on Robbins Reef." *New York Times,* March 5, 1906, section 3, 7.

CHAPTER THREE: *The Lady on the Lake*

"A Fragile Woman of 80 Years Is Uncle Sam's Oldest and Most Reliable Lighthouse Keeper." *Chicago Tribune* (October 2, 1904).

Harris, Patricia. "Indiana's Only Lighthouse." *The Keeper's Log* (Summer 1987).

"Lighthouse Story." *Old Lighthouse Museum News* 15, no. 2 (June 1989).

The Michigan City Evening News
    "Another Old Resident Answers Death's Call." April 16, 1905.
    "Funeral of Miss Colfax." April 1905.
    "Gone to Her Reward." April 1905.
    "Letter from Miss Colfax." October 14, 1904.

Molloy, Emma Barrett. "The Temperance Track." *Elkhart Observer* (April 22, 1874).

Warnes, Kathleen. "Lighthouse Luminaries on the Great Lakes." *Inland Seas* 42, no. 3 (Fall 1986).

CHAPTER FOUR: *The Grandes Dames of Lightkeeping*

Gallant, Clifford. "Emily Fish, The Socialite Keeper." *The Keeper's Log* (Spring 1985).

Holland, Francis Ross. *America's Lighthouses: Their Illustrated History Since 1716.* Brattleboro, Vt.: Stephen Grune Press, 1972.

Lists of Lights and Fog Signals. Washington, D.C.: Department of Commerce Printing, 1939.

Shanks, Ralph. *Guardians of the Golden Gate.* Petaluma, Calif.: Costano Books, 1990.

_____. *Lighthouses and Lightboat Stations of San Francisco.* San Anselmo, Calif.: Costano Books, 1978.

CHAPTER FIVE: *Other Legendary Ladies of the Light*

ABBIE BURGESS

Holland, Francis Ross. *America's Lighthouses: Their Illustrated History Since 1716.* Brattleboro, Vt.: Stephen Grune Press, 1972.

Roop, Peter, and Connie Roop. *Keep the Lights Burning, Abbie.* Minneapolis: Carolrhoda Books, 1985.

Snow, Edward Rowe. *The Lighthouses of New England.* New York: Dodd, Mead & Company, 1945.

LAURA HECOX

Francis, Philip. "Beautiful Santa Cruz County." Pamphlet written for Santa Cruz County, California, 1896.

Perry, Frank. "California's Lighthouse Keeper Naturalist." *Pacific Discovery* 33, no. 5 (September–October 1980).

_____. *Lighthouse Point: Reflections on Monterey Bay History.* Soquel, Calif.: GBH Publishing, 1982.

Rowland, Leon. *Santa Cruz: The Early Years.* Santa Cruz, Calif.: Paper Vision Press, 1980.

MARY REYNOLDS

Clifford, Mary Louise, and J. Candace Clifford. *Women Who Kept the Lights: An Illustrated History of Female Lighthouse Keepers.* Williamsburg, Va.: Cypress Communications, 1993.

MARIA AND MIRANDA YOUNGHANS

Dewire, Elinor. "Women Lighthouse Keepers." *American History Illustrated* 21 (February 1987).

Holland, Francis Ross. *America's Lighthouses: Their Illustrated History Since 1716.* Brattleboro, Vt.: Stephen Grune Press, 1972.

Jones, Ray, and Bruce Roberts. *Southern Lighthouses, Chesapeake Bay to the Gulf of Mexico.* Chester, Conn.: Globe Pequot Press, 1989.

FANNIE SALTER

Dewire, Elinor. "Women Lighthouse Keepers." *American History Illustrated* 21 (February 1987).

Jones, Ray, and Bruce Roberts. *Southern Lighthouses, Chesapeake Bay to the Gulf of Mexico.* Chester, Conn.: Globe Pequot Press, 1989.

Lists of Lights and Fog Signals. Washington, D.C.: Department of Commerce Printing, 1939.

INDEX

Boldface pages are illustrations

Photo Credits